Essential COOKING SERIES

COMPREHENSIVE, STEP BY STEP COOKING

Casseroles
& Stews

BUDGET
BOOKS

Food Editor: Neil Hargreaves
Cover Design: Budget Books
Prepress: Graphic Print Group

 BUDGET Essential Cooking Series: Casseroles & Stews
B First published in 2008 by Budget Books Pty Ltd
BOOKS 45–55 Fairchild Street
Heatherton, Victoria, 3202, Australia

10 9 8 7 6 5
13 12 11 10 09

Disclaimer: The nutritional information listed under each recipe does not
include the nutrient content of garnishes or any accompaniments not listed
in specific quantitites in the ingredient list. The nutritional information for
each recipe is an estimate only, and may vary depending on the brand of
ingredients used, and due to natural biological variations in the composition
of natural foods such as meat, fish, fruit and vegetables. The nutritional
information was calculated by using Foodworks dietary analysis software
(Version 3, Xyris Software Pty Ltd, Highgate Hill, Queensland, Australia) based
on the Australian food composition tables and food manufacturers' data.
Where not specified, ingredients are always analysed as average or medium,
not small or large.

ISBN: 978 1 7418 1465 1

Printed and bound in China

Contents

An introduction to casserole dishes

It's strange to think that the words 'casserole' and 'stew' mean exactly the same, for they conjure up two entirely different concepts in most people's minds. One thinks of a casserole as being French and exotic, rich in flavour and served in an attractive dish. A stew, on the other hand, brings to mind frugal cuts of meat which, cooked in any other way, might well be tough. Some of us possibly remember Irish stew as being a little lacklustre and basic, but there is no reason why it shouldn't be as flavoursome as any exciting French casserole.

The essence of casserole dishes is the relatively slow cooking of a mixture of ingredients and a small amount of liquid, in a dish which has a close-fitting lid. The fit of the lid is important, as it ensures the richness of the result and minimal loss of liquid. Ideally, too, the casserole dish should distribute heat well and evenly, so that food doesn't stick on the bottom. This is why the enamelled cast-iron casserole dishes are so popular. China, pottery, earthenware and heat-resistant glass are all satisfactory, although much more fragile; and it is not a good thing to have any cracks in dishes, as they not only harbour germs but often allow liquids to escape. Nowadays the range and choice of casserole dishes are marvellous and can add enormously to the look of the table and the pleasure of eating. Before using a particular type of dish, check first that it is suitable for the method of cooking chosen. Some are not suitable for cooking on top of the stove, so care must be taken.

Cooking very slowly is useful if you are likely to be away from the kitchen and is also good for the tougher cuts of meat, which need very slow cooking. Going back to the old-fashioned way of doing things can be a new and rewarding experience.

TIPS FOR THE FREEZER

Frozen meat must be thawed if the recipe states that the meat must first be browned. All poultry and game must be thawed before they are used in any type of cooked dish, as bacteria can lurk near the bone. Cooked casseroles can be reheated directly from the frozen state and a quantity for four people will take 1 to 1½ hours to reheat thoroughly at 160°C.

Some silicone containers can be used in the freezer and are suitable for using direct from freezer to oven. This also applies to foil containers and metal containers. However, few of us have enough casserole dishes to leave the meat in the containers. The best way is to freeze it in the casserole dish, then turn it out into a large zip-lock plastic freezer bag. Label each casserole with the date and the description of the casserole and it can then be put back into the same casserole dish for reheating without any difficulty. Casseroles flavoured with herbs, wine and spices do tend to change flavour in the freezer. Over 3 to 4 weeks this is not too

noticeable but over several months you may find that you have to adjust the flavourings when reheating. A good tip to remember for casseroles to be frozen is to undercook them by half an hour. Few foods freeze as easily or as well as casseroles. The factor that determines successful casserole freezing is the thickening agent. If the casserole is thickened simply by cooking it down until the liquid in it is of a substantial consistency, then the stew can be frozen with no special precautions.

Casseroles thickened with flour or cornflour may break down and separate after freezing. If you plan to freeze such a stew to serve later, substitute rice flour tablespoon for tablespoon for flour or 2 tablespoons to 1 for cornflour. If casseroles contain tender green vegetables, both the colour and texture will be much better if you add the vegetables after defrosting and reheating. Use frozen casseroles within four to six months of storing them. A good tip for bones (beef, chicken or whatever) is to seal them in heavy plastic bags and freeze them until you are ready to make casseroles and broths.

COOKING IN QUANTITES

Cooking meat in bulk for casseroles pays dividends in time and kitchen mess. Large quantities of beef, lamb, pork or veal can be browned at one session, casseroled with chopped onions and seasoning for 1 hour, then divided into 2, 4, 6 or 8 portions. Prepare vegetables and herbs and cook as for a freshly made casserole.

COOKING TIMES

Cooking times for casseroles depend very much on the quality of meat used and, to some extent, on the casserole dish itself, so always test your casserole at the minimum time given to make sure the meat does not become overcooked.

VERSATILE DISH

Casseroles are interesting and creative to make, as the flavour can always be varied to suit the mood of the cook. Basically meat or poultry, vegetables, herbs, seasoning and stock are the ingredients. A change of herb or vegetable can transform the basic brown stew or chicken casserole into an exciting meal to suit the individual tastes of each family. There was a time when the chicken that went into the stewpot was a stewing hen – an ample bird of a certain age. These days, unless you shop at a special poultry store, it's hard to find such flavourful chickens. But you can still achieve rich-tasting stews with a young frying chicken weighing 2 kilograms or more. There is an astonishing variety of fish and shellfish, and many markets offer a good selection of whole and filleted fish to use in the recipes that follow. Vegetables and pulses also make worthy casseroles; combining root vegetables with fresh herbs, lentils or chickpeas is the foundation of many a good vegetarian meal.

Many of the world's great dishes are casseroled meats and vegetables cooked slowly in a well-seasoned liquid until they are tender, moist and irresistible. Every country has at least one stew that could be considered a national dish – indeed, a national treasure. Most of these stews require a fair amount of cooking time. But once you have them safely simmering, you can usually ignore them while you attend to other matters. Nothing makes a kitchen smell and feel more like the days of old than a bubbling casserole.

Georgian lamb stew

INGREDIENTS

700 g chump chops
1 large onion, chopped
2 cups canned peeled tomatoes,
 drained
2 kg potatoes, peeled and cut into
 2 cm pieces
salt and freshly ground black pepper
$\frac{1}{2}$ cup coarsely chopped fresh
 coriander, mint leaves, basil leaves,
 parsley leaves and dill sprigs
$\frac{1}{2}$ teaspoon cayenne pepper
4 cloves garlic, crushed
serves 4

PREPARATION TIME
20 minutes

COOKING TIME
1 hour 15 minutes

1 Remove the bones and cut the lamb into large pieces.

2 In a large saucepan, cook the lamb over low heat, stirring frequently, for 10
minutes or until browned on all sides. Add onion and cook over a moderately
low heat, stirring occasionally, until the onion is softened. Add the tomatoes
(breaking them up with a wooden spoon), potatoes and a pinch of salt and
pepper and simmer, half-covered, stirring occasionally, for 40 minutes or
until the lamb and potatoes are tender.

3 Add the herb mixture and cayenne pepper and simmer, stirring, for a further
4 minutes. Stir in the garlic and remove the stew from the heat. Let it stand,
covered, for 5 minutes and season it with salt and pepper before serving.

NUTRITIONAL VALUE PER SERVE   FAT **19.5** G   CARBOHYDRATE **72** G   PROTEIN **48** G

Lamb hotpot

INGREDIENTS

40 g flour
salt and freshly ground black pepper
750 g lamb leg cut into 3 cm cubes
¼ cup olive oil
1 bunch spring onions, trimmed,
    halved
3 cloves garlic, freshly crushed
3 bacon rashers, roughly chopped
⅓ cup white wine
2 cups chicken stock
3 bay leaves
2 teaspoons rosemary leaves, dried
2 tablespoons tomato paste
350 g baby potatoes, halved
1 cup peas, shelled
1 large carrot, peeled, halved, sliced
2 tablespoons parsley leaves,
    chopped
serves 4

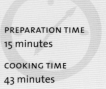

PREPARATION TIME
15 minutes

COOKING TIME
43 minutes

1 Combine the flour, salt and pepper on a large plate. Dip the lamb pieces lightly in the flour.

2 Heat 1 tablespoon olive oil in a large saucepan over high heat. Add the lamb in two batches and cook for 3–4 minutes or until brown. Remove the lamb and set aside.

3 Heat the remaining oil. Add the spring onions and cook for 3 minutes. Add the garlic and bacon and cook for a further 2 minutes. Add the wine, chicken stock, herbs, tomato paste, baby potatoes and lamb. Bring to the boil, cover and simmer for 20 minutes. Add the peas and carrot and simmer uncovered for a further 10 minutes. Stir the parsley through and serve.

NUTRITIONAL VALUE PER SERVE	FAT 26 G	CARBOHYDRATE 32 G	PROTEIN 40 G

Slow-simmered lamb shanks with couscous

INGREDIENTS

2 tablespoons canola oil
4 frenched lamb shanks
  (ask your butcher to do this)
2 cups canned chopped tomatoes
1 cup red wine
1 bay leaf
6 sprigs fresh thyme
1 cinnamon stick
1½ cups pumpkin, cut into large
  pieces
2 zucchinis, cut into large pieces
8 dried apricots
8 dried prunes
1 cup couscous
2 cups boiling water
2 tablespoons flaked almonds,
  toasted

serves 4

PREPARATION TIME
15 minutes

COOKING TIME
1 hour 40 minutes

1 Preheat the oven to 175°C. Heat oil in a large frying pan over a high heat and sear the lamb shanks in batches until browned all over. Transfer to an ovenproof casserole dish.

2 Add the tomatoes, wine, bay leaf, thyme and cinnamon stick. Cover and bake for 1 hour. Add the pumpkin, zucchini, apricots and prunes and cook uncovered for 30 minutes or until the vegetables are soft and the lamb starts to come away from the bone.

3 Put the couscous into a large bowl, cover with 2 cups of boiling water and allow it to stand for 10 minutes or until all the liquid is absorbed.

4 Serve the lamb shanks in deep bowls on top of the couscous and garnish with the flaked almonds.

NUTRITIONAL VALUE PER SERVE   FAT 17 G   CARBOHYDRATE 56 G   PROTEIN 40.5 G

Slow-cooked lamb and macadamias

INGREDIENTS

700 g boneless leg lamb, trimmed
  of visible fat, cut into 2 cm cubes
⅓ cup raisins
½ cup evaporated skim milk
spicy yoghurt marinade
1 white onion, diced
⅓ cup ground unsalted macadamias
2 cm piece fresh ginger, chopped
½ cup low-fat plain yoghurt
3 teaspoons ground coriander
2 teaspoons ground cardamom
½ teaspoon freshly ground black
  pepper
serves 4

PREPARATION TIME
15 minutes

COOKING TIME
2 hours

1 To make the marinade, place the onion, macadamias, ginger and yoghurt in a food processor. Process to combine. Stir in coriander, cardamom and pepper.

2 Place the lamb in a non-reactive dish. Pour over the marinade and toss to coat. Cover and marinate in the refrigerator overnight.

3 Transfer the meat mixture to a heavy-based saucepan. Stir in the raisins and evaporated milk. Place the pan over a medium heat and bring to a simmer. Reduce the heat to low. Cover and cook, stirring occasionally, for 1½ hours.

4 Remove cover. Cook, stirring occasionally, for 30–40 minutes or until meat is tender and the sauce is thick. Add a little water during cooking, if necessary.

5 Serve with boiled rice and steamed vegetables of your choice.

NUTRITIONAL VALUE PER SERVE	FAT 20 G	CARBOHYDRATE 17 G	PROTEIN 46.5 G

Lemon and thyme lamb

INGREDIENTS

750 g lean diced lamb forequarter
1 tablespoon olive oil
1 tablespoon thyme leaves
2 teaspoons garlic, crushed
1 onion, chopped
¼ cup plain flour
¼ cup lemon juice
¼ cup sweet white wine
¾ cup chicken stock
freshly ground black pepper
1 sprig fresh thyme
serves 4–6

1 Preheat oven to 160°C. Combine lamb, oil, thyme and garlic. Brown lamb in pan with onion. Add flour and cook for 5 minutes. Pour in lemon juice, wine and stock.

2 Cover and simmer 1½ hours, stirring occasionally, or bake in covered ovenproof dish for 1½ hours. Season with pepper.

3 Garnish with pieces of fresh thyme and serve immediately.

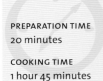

PREPARATION TIME
20 minutes

COOKING TIME
1 hour 45 minutes

NUTRITIONAL VALUE PER SERVE	FAT 13.5 G	CARBOHYDRATE 59 G	PROTEIN 38 G

Lamb and prune tagine

INGREDIENTS

2 tablespoons olive oil
400 g lamb, cut into 2 cm cubes
1 onion, finely chopped
$\frac{1}{2}$ teaspoon ground ginger
1$\frac{1}{2}$ cups chicken stock
1 cinnamon stick
salt and freshly ground black pepper
   to taste
1 cup pitted prunes
1 tablespoon honey
2 teaspoons grated orange rind
1 cup couscous
2 cups boiling water
serves 4

1 Heat oil in a saucepan over a high heat, add the lamb cubes and onion and spread in a single layer. When the underside of the lamb has changed colour, turn over to sear and seal all sides, tossing at intervals. Add the ginger, stir to coat the meat and pour in the stock. Add the cinnamon stick, salt and pepper. Bring to the boil, immediately reduce the heat and simmer for 50 minutes.

2 Stir in the prunes, honey and orange rind. Simmer, covered, for 40 minutes or until the lamb is tender. Remove the lid to reduce the liquid content for the last 10 minutes of cooking.

3 Put the couscous into a large bowl, cover with 2 cups of boiling water and allow it to stand for 10 minutes or until all the liquid is absorbed. Serve casserole over steamed couscous.

PREPARATION TIME
20 minutes

COOKING TIME
2 hours

| NUTRITIONAL VALUE PER SERVE | FAT 13.5 G | CARBOHYDRATE 28 G | PROTEIN 21.5 G |

Lamb casserole with couscous and gremolata

INGREDIENTS

2 tablespoons plain flour
salt and freshly ground black pepper
650 g diced lamb
2–3 tablespoons olive oil
1 yellow and 1 green capsicum,
   deseeded and chopped
2 cups canned chopped tomatoes
gremolata
1 clove garlic, very finely chopped
3 tablespoons fresh parsley, chopped
zest of 1 lemon
couscous
2 cups couscous
2 cups boiling water
1 tablespoon olive oil
1 onion, finely sliced
serves 4

PREPARATION TIME
30 minutes

COOKING TIME
1 hour

1 Preheat the oven to 175°C. Season the flour and spread it on a large plate, then toss the meat in the seasoned flour until coated. Heat the oil in a large frying pan and cook the meat over a medium heat for 2–3 minutes each side, until browned (you will need to do this in 2 batches). Transfer the browned meat to a casserole dish.

2 Add the capsicums to the frying pan and cook for 2 minutes. Add the tomatoes and bring to the boil. Add these to the lamb and cook in the oven for 40 minutes or until the meat is tender. Meanwhile, mix all the gremolata ingredients together.

3 Put the couscous into a large bowl, cover with 2 cups of boiling water and allow it to stand for 10 minutes or until all the liquid is absorbed.

4 Heat oil in a small frying pan and cook the onion over a medium heat for 10 minutes until golden brown. Add to couscous and mix well. Sprinkle the gremolata over the lamb and serve with the couscous.

NUTRITIONAL VALUE PER SERVE	FAT 24 G	CARBOHYDRATE 49 G	PROTEIN 52.5 G

Lamb and apricot stew

INGREDIENTS

3 ripe tomatoes, blanched and peeled
2 tablespoons oil
1 small green capsicum, seeded and
  finely chopped
1 small onion, chopped
1 tablespoon fresh mint, chopped
650 g lamb cubes, cut from the leg or
  shoulder
½ cup dried apricots
salt and freshly ground black pepper
serves 4

PREPARATION TIME
15 minutes

COOKING TIME
2 hours 20 minutes

1 Cut the tomatoes in half crosswise (through the 'equator'), gently squeeze out the seeds and chop the tomatoes.

2 Heat half the oil in a heavy-based, lidded frying pan or saucepan, add the tomatoes, capsicum, onion and mint and fry for 5 minutes. Remove from the pan.

3 Heat the remaining oil, add the lamb and stir it quickly to brown on all sides. Return the vegetables to the pan and add the apricots and enough water to almost cover the meat. Bring to the boil, turn down the heat, and simmer for 1 hour.

4 Season with salt and pepper. Check the liquid content and add more water if needed. Simmer 1 hour more, until the lamb is very tender. May be served with boiled rice.

NUTRITIONAL VALUE PER SERVE	FAT 37 G	CARBOHYDRATE 11 G	PROTEIN 48 G

Beef braised in rioja

INGREDIENTS

3 tablespoons olive oil
700 g stewing beef, cut into 6 cm
    cubes
2 cloves garlic, crushed
6 shallots, finely chopped
2 sticks celery, thickly sliced
1½ cups mushrooms, thickly sliced
½ teaspoon ground allspice
½ bottle full-bodied red wine
1 cup tomato purée
2 sprigs fresh thyme
salt and freshly ground black pepper
serves 4

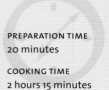

PREPARATION TIME
20 minutes

COOKING TIME
2 hours 15 minutes

1 Preheat the oven to 160°C. Heat the oil in a frying pan or a large saucepan and fry the meat over a high heat, stirring, for 5–10 minutes until browned. Remove from the pan, then add the shallots, garlic and celery. Cook, stirring, for 3–4 minutes, until lightly browned.

2 Add the mushrooms and cook for 1 minute or until softened. Stir in the allspice, wine, tomato purée, 1 sprig of thyme and salt and pepper. Return the meat to the dish or pan and bring the mixture to a simmer.

3 Cover and cook in the oven or over a low heat on the stove for 1½–2 hours, until the beef is tender. Season again if necessary, and garnish with the remaining thyme. Serve with rice or mashed potato.

NUTRITIONAL VALUE PER SERVE	FAT 22 G	CARBOHYDRATE 5 G	PROTEIN 39 G

Rich beef stew with shallots

INGREDIENTS

4 shallots, quartered
4 large cloves garlic, quartered
2 large carrots, sliced
3 sticks celery, sliced
3 tablespoons olive oil
800 g lean stewing beef, cut into
   5 cm cubes
a few thyme sprigs, 1 bay leaf,
   1 rosemary sprig and 1 strip of
   lemon rind, tied with string
1½ cups full-bodied red wine
½ cup beef stock
2 tablespoons pearl barley
6 black peppercorns, crushed
salt and freshly ground black pepper
serves 4

PREPARATION TIME
20 minutes

COOKING TIME
3 hours 10 minutes

1 Place the shallots, garlic, carrots and celery in a large frying pan and pour over 2 tablespoons of oil. Cook for 15 minutes, on a medium heat, turning frequently. Set aside.

2 Add the remaining oil to the frying pan, then add a third of the meat and fry for 5–8 minutes. Remove from the pan while you cook the remaining meat in 2 more batches. Return all the meat to the frying pan. Add the vegetables, herb bundle, wine, stock, barley and peppercorns. Season with salt and pepper and bring to the boil.

3 Reduce the heat and simmer, partly covered, for 2–2½ hours, until the meat is tender. Check from time to time and add a little more stock or water if the stew starts to dry out. Remove the herb bundle before serving.

NUTRITIONAL VALUE PER SERVE	FAT 22 G	CARBOHYDRATE 8 G	PROTEIN 45.5 G

Beef curry

INGREDIENTS

1½ kg blade beef
salt and freshly ground black pepper
2 tablespoons oil
1 brown onion, finely chopped
2 cloves garlic, finely chopped
1 tablespoon curry paste
¼ teaspoon ground ginger
¼ teaspoon turmeric
⅛ teaspoon chilli powder
2 tablespoons plain flour
1¼ cups beef stock
½ cup yoghurt
1 tablespoon lemon juice
lemon or lime wedges, to garnish
serves 4–6

1 Cut beef into 3 cm cubes. Season the beef with salt and pepper.

2 Heat the oil in a large, heavy-based saucepan, add a third of the beef and brown well on all sides. Remove and brown the remaining beef in 2 batches. Remove from pan.

3 Add the onion and garlic and fry until translucent. Stir in the curry paste, spices and flour and cook for 1 minute. Add the stock and beef. Cover with a lid and simmer gently until the beef is very tender, around 1 hour, stirring occasionally.

4 Stir in the yoghurt and lemon juice. Serve topped with lemon or lime wedges.

PREPARATION TIME
10 minutes

COOKING TIME
2 hours

| NUTRITIONAL VALUE PER SERVE | FAT 26 G | CARBOHYDRATE 6.5 G | PROTEIN 87 G |

Spanish beef stew

INGREDIENTS

3 tablespoons olive oil
680 g stewing beef, trimmed of fat
   and cut into 5 cm chunks
2 medium onions, finely chopped
2 cloves garlic, crushed
1 stick celery, thickly sliced
$\frac{1}{2}$ teaspoon smoked paprika
1 anchovy
$\frac{1}{2}$ cup dry white wine
1 zucchini, finely diced
250 g mushrooms, thickly sliced
1 cup red wine
1 cup tomato purée
2 sprigs fresh thyme
salt and freshly ground black pepper
serves 4

1 Preheat the oven to 180°C. Heat oil in a large saucepan and fry meat over a high heat, stirring, for 6 minutes, until browned. Remove from the pan and set aside.

2 Add onions, garlic, celery, paprika and anchovy. Cook for 5 minutes, stirring occasionally. Add the white wine to the saucepan and turn contents into a casserole dish.

3 Add zucchini, mushrooms red wine, tomato purée and thyme to the casserole dish. Season with salt and pepper. Add meat to the dish, cover and cook in the oven 1$\frac{1}{2}$–2 hours, until beef is tender.

PREPARATION TIME
25 minutes

COOKING TIME
approximately 2 hours

NUTRITIONAL VALUE PER SERVE	FAT **24** G	CARBOHYDRATE **16** G	PROTEIN **55** G

Steak and kidney puffs

INGREDIENTS

2–4 tablespoons peanut oil
1 onion, finely chopped
500 g braising steak, cut into cubes
350 g lamb kidney, halved, cores
  removed and cut into 1 cm pieces
3 tablespoons plain flour
1 tablespoon tomato paste
2 teaspoons Worcestershire sauce
1½ cups beef stock
finely grated zest of 1 lemon
4 tablespoons fresh parsley, finely
  chopped
1 teaspoon dried mixed herbs
salt and freshly ground black pepper
½ cup baby button mushrooms
1 pack ready-rolled puff pastry
fresh rosemary
serves 4

PREPARATION TIME
20 minutes

COOKING TIME
2 hours 50 minutes

1 Preheat the oven to 160°C. Heat 2 tablespoons of the oil in a large frying pan that can be placed in the oven, add the onion and cook for 5 minutes. Add half the steak and kidney and fry over a high heat, stirring, for 6 minutes or until browned. Remove from the pan and keep warm. Fry the remaining meat, adding more oil if necessary.

2 Return all the meat to the dish, add the flour and stir for 2 minutes. Add the tomato paste, Worcestershire sauce, stock, lemon zest, 2 tablespoons of the parsley, herbs, salt and pepper. Bring to boil, stirring, then cover.

3 Transfer to the oven. After 1½ hours, stir in the mushrooms and a little water, if needed. Cook for 35 minutes more. Meanwhile, unroll the pastry and cut it into 4 x 11 cm circles. Put them on a greased baking sheet.

4 Take the casserole out of the oven. Increase the temperature to 200°C. Bake the pastry for 15 minutes. Top each pastry circle with the steak and kidney, and return to the oven for 5 minutes. Garnish with the remaining chopped parsley and rosemary.

NUTRITIONAL VALUE PER SERVE	FAT 31.5 G	CARBOHYDRATE 24 G	PROTEIN 46.5 G

Jarkoy

INGREDIENTS

2 tablespoons butter or oil
750 g thick-cut steak, cut into large
  cubes
2 large carrots, thinly sliced
2 medium onions, thinly sliced
1 tablespoon plain flour
2 cloves garlic, crushed
1 teaspoon chopped fresh dill or
  $\frac{1}{2}$ teaspoon dried dill
$\frac{1}{2}$ teaspoon nutmeg, grated or
  ground
salt and freshly ground black pepper
$\frac{1}{3}$ cup beef stock
$\frac{1}{2}$ cup dried apricots
$\frac{1}{2}$ cup pitted prunes
1 teaspoon mint, chopped
1 tablespoon coriander, chopped
$\frac{1}{2}$ cup walnuts, crushed
$\frac{1}{4}$ cup orange juice
serves 4

PREPARATION TIME
20 minutes

COOKING TIME
2 hours 30 minutes

1 Heat the butter or oil in a large heavy-based saucepan over high heat and add $\frac{1}{3}$ of
   the beef cubes. Toss to brown well on all sides. Remove and brown the remaining
   2 batches. Add the carrots and onions and fry a little.

2 Return all the meat to the saucepan and sprinkle in the flour to cover the surface.
   Add the garlic, dill, nutmeg, salt, pepper and stock. Bring to the boil over a high heat,
   stirring to lift the browned-on juices. Cover, reduce the heat to low and simmer
   slowly for $1\frac{1}{2}$ hours.

3 Add dried apricots, prunes, mint and coriander. Cover and simmer 30 minutes more,
   or until the meat is tender. Serve sprinkled with walnuts and orange juice.

| NUTRITIONAL VALUE PER SERVE | FAT 22 G | CARBOHYDRATE 26 G | PROTEIN 52 G |

Lovely legs and vegetable casserole

INGREDIENTS

340 g tomato sauce
$^1/_2$ cup water
$^1/_4$ cup prepared basil pesto
1 kg chicken drumsticks
4 medium potatoes, peeled and
   quartered
2 tablespoons olive oil
2 tablespoons parsley, finely chopped
1$^1/_2$ cups frozen peas
1$^1/_2$ cups canned baby corn
serves 4

PREPARATION TIME
5 minutes

COOKING TIME
55 minutes

1 Preheat the oven to 180°C. Pour the tomato sauce into a casserole or baking dish and stir in the water and pesto. Place the chicken drumsticks in 1 layer and arrange the potato quarters in between. Drizzle over the olive oil and sprinkle with the parsley. Cover with foil.

2 Place the dish in the oven and cook for 30 minutes. Remove from the oven and turn the chicken and potatoes. Add the peas and baby corn. Return to the oven and cook, uncovered, for 25 minutes more or until the chicken and potatoes are tender when tested.

3 Serve with crusty bread.

| NUTRITIONAL VALUE PER SERVE | FAT 52.5 G | CARBOHYDRATE 26 G | PROTEIN 49 G |

Light chicken curry

INGREDIENTS

2 cups reduced-fat coconut milk
1 cup reduced-salt chicken stock
2–3 tablespoons green curry paste
3 kaffir lime leaves, finely shredded
1½ cups pumpkin, peeled and
  chopped
4 skinless chicken breast fillets, cut
  into small cubes
canned bamboo shoots, drained
1 cup snake beans, chopped
1 cup broccoli, cut into florets
1 tablespoon fish sauce
1 tablespoon palm sugar, grated
2 tablespoons Thai basil leaves, torn
serves 4

PREPARATION TIME
15 minutes

COOKING TIME
30 minutes

1 Put the coconut milk, stock, curry paste and lime leaves into a wok
  or large pot and bring to the boil. Cook over a high heat until the
  sauce starts to thicken slightly. Add the pumpkin and simmer for
  10 minutes, or until it starts to soften.

2 Add the chicken and bamboo shoots, reduce the heat and simmer
  for 10 minutes or until the chicken is tender. Add the beans,
  broccoli, fish sauce and palm sugar and cook, uncovered, until the
  vegetables are soft.

3 Remove from the heat and stir through the basil leaves. Serve
  with jasmine rice on the side.

NUTRITIONAL VALUE PER SERVE	FAT 37 G	CARBOHYDRATE 74 G	PROTEIN 85 G

Drumsticks in dill sauce

INGREDIENTS

2 tablespoons butter
700 g chicken drumsticks
²/₃ cup spring onions, chopped
2 tablespoons dill, chopped
¼ cup lemon juice
½ teaspoon salt
¼ teaspoon white pepper
1 small bunch carrots, peeled
2 cups water
1 chicken stock cube
2 tablespoons cornflour
2 tablespoons water, extra
serves 4

PREPARATION TIME
5 minutes

COOKING TIME
approximately 1 hour

1 Heat the butter in a heavy-based saucepan. Add the drumsticks a few at a time and brown lightly on all sides. Remove to a plate.

2 Add the spring onions and fry for 1 minute. Stir in half of the dill. Add the lemon juice, return the drumsticks to the saucepan and sprinkle with the salt and pepper.

3 Arrange the carrots over the drumsticks. Add the combined water and stock cube. Bring to a simmer, turn down the heat, and cover and simmer for 40 minutes until tender.

4 Remove the drumsticks and carrots with a slotted spoon and arrange on a heated platter. Blend the cornflour with water and stir into the juices remaining in the pan. Stir over heat until the sauce boils and thickens. Pour over the drumsticks and carrots. Serve topped with the remaining dill.

NUTRITIONAL VALUE PER SERVE   FAT **16** G   CARBOHYDRATE **6** G   PROTEIN **32** G

Coq au vin

INGREDIENTS

1½ kg chicken pieces
½ cup seasoned flour
1 tablespoon olive oil
2 cloves garlic, crushed
8 pickling onions or shallots, peeled
6 rashers bacon, chopped
⅔ cup chicken stock
3 cups red wine
1 cup button mushrooms
freshly ground black pepper
serves 4–6

1 Toss the chicken in flour to coat. Shake off the excess flour and set aside.

2 Heat the oil in a large frying pan over a medium heat and cook the chicken in batches, turning frequently, for 10 minutes or until brown on all sides. Remove the chicken from the pan and drain on kitchen towel.

3 Add the garlic, onions or shallots, and bacon to the pan and cook, stirring, for 5 minutes or until the onions are golden. Return the chicken to the pan, stir in the stock and wine and bring to the boil. Reduce the heat, cover and simmer, stirring occasionally, for 1¼ hours or until the chicken is tender. Add the mushrooms and pepper to taste and cook for 10 minutes longer.

PREPARATION TIME
5 minutes

COOKING TIME
1 hour 50 minutes

| NUTRITIONAL VALUE PER SERVE | FAT 27 G | CARBOHYDRATE 11 G | PROTEIN 84.5 G |

Coconut cashew chicken

INGREDIENTS

¼ cup cashews
2 tablespoons butter
2 cloves garlic, crushed
2 small onions, finely chopped
1 tablespoon fresh ginger, grated
1 tablespoon ground coriander
1 teaspoon tumeric powder
½ teaspoon ground nutmeg
450 g boneless chicken thigh or
  breast fillets, cut into 2 cm cubes
1 tablespoon double cream
2 cups coconut milk
2 tablespoons coriander leaves
serves 4

1 To roast the cashews, spread them over a baking tray and bake for 5–10 minutes, or until lightly and evenly browned. Toss back and forth occasionally with a spoon to ensure even browning.

2 Melt the butter in a saucepan over a medium heat, add the garlic, onions and ginger, cook, stirring, for 3 minutes or until the onions are golden.

3 Stir in the spices and cook for 2 minutes until fragrant. Add the chicken and cook, stirring, for 5 minutes or until the chicken is brown.

4 Add the cashews, cream and coconut milk, bring to simmering point and simmer, stirring occasionally, for 35 minutes. Serve on a bed of rice and garnish with coriander.

PREPARATION TIME
10 minutes

COOKING TIME
1 hour

| NUTRITIONAL VALUE PER SERVE | FAT 81.5 G | CARBOHYDRATE 6 G | PROTEIN 26 G |

Chicken cacciatore

INGREDIENTS

1 kg chicken breast fillets
4 tablespoons seasoned plain flour
4 tablespoons olive oil
1 green capsicum, diced
1 medium onion, finely chopped
2 cloves garlic, crushed
425 g canned tomatoes
1 tablespoon tomato paste
1 bay leaf
1 teaspoon oregano
1 teaspoon sugar
¼ cup dry white wine
¼ cup marsala
2 tablespoons parsley, chopped
10 black olives, to garnish
serves 4

PREPARATION TIME
15 minutes

COOKING TIME
approximately 1 hour

1 Cut each breast fillet into 2 or 3 pieces and coat well with seasoned flour.

2 Heat oil to hot in a heavy-based saucepan and fry chicken a few pieces at a time until golden brown on all sides. Remove to a plate. Drain oil from the pan, leaving about 1 tablespoon.

3 Add capsicum, onion and garlic and fry for 3 minutes. Chop the tomatoes and add with their juice; add tomato paste, bay leaf, oregano and sugar. Bring to the boil, reduce heat, and simmer for 5 minutes. Return chicken to the pan, add wine and marsala and parsley, cover and simmer slowly for 35 minutes.

4 Serve on a bed of fettucine and top with olives to garnish.

NUTRITIONAL VALUE PER SERVE	FAT 26 G	CARBOHYDRATE 14 G	PROTEIN 45.5 G

Chicken gumbo

INGREDIENTS

6 tablespoons butter
6–8 chicken thighs, legs or wings
500 g okra
1 large onion, finely chopped
1 clove garlic, crushed
250 g ham, cut in 1 thick slice,
 then cubed
1 red capsicum, seeded and cubed
1½ cups peeled, chopped tomatoes
1 tablespoon tomato paste
½ cup dry white wine or chicken
 stock
1 bay leaf
salt and freshly ground black pepper
cayenne pepper or tabasco sauce
2 tablespoons chopped parsley
serves 4

PREPARATION TIME
6 minutes

COOKING TIME
approximately 1 hour

1 Melt the butter in a deep frying pan, add the chicken and brown
  on all sides. Remove and keep warm. Add the okra, onion, garlic,
  ham and capsicum to the pan and stir-fry until the onion is soft.

2 Add the tomatoes, tomato paste, wine or stock, bay leaf, salt,
  pepper and cayenne pepper or tabasco sauce to taste.

3 Add the chicken to the pan, cover and simmer for 40 minutes until
  the chicken is tender. Garnish with chopped parsley and serve.

NUTRITIONAL VALUE PER SERVE	FAT 56 G	CARBOHYDRATE 10 G	PROTEIN 94 G

Rich fish stew

INGREDIENTS

2 teaspoons olive oil
1 leek, chopped
1 clove garlic, crushed
1 teaspoon ground oregano
4 flat mushrooms, sliced
1 stalk celery, sliced
2 zucchinis, sliced
1 tablespoon tomato paste
2 cups canned diced tomatoes
$^1/_2$ cup white wine
455 g firm white fish fillets, such as
  gemfish, ling, barramundi, sea bass
  or blue-eye cod
1 tablespoon fresh basil, chopped
1 tablespoon fresh parsley, chopped
sprig rosemary, to garnish
serves 4

PREPARATION TIME
20 minutes

COOKING TIME
30 minutes

1 Heat the oil in a deep frying pan over a medium heat. Add the leek and
   garlic. Cook, stirring, for 1–2 minutes or until soft. Add the oregano,
   mushrooms and celery. Cook, stirring, for 2–3 minutes.

2 Stir in the zucchini, tomato paste, tomatoes and wine. Bring to the boil.
   Reduce the heat and simmer, stirring occasionally, for 5 minutes or until the
   mixture starts to thicken.

3 Add the fish. Cook for 6 minutes or until the fish is just cooked; take care
   not to overcook or the fish will fall apart. Stir in the basil and parsley. Serve
   with mashed potato and a sprig of rosemary.

NUTRITIONAL VALUE PER SERVE	FAT 13.5 G	CARBOHYDRATE 16 G	PROTEIN 29 G

Chilli mud crab stew

INGREDIENTS

2 small red chillies, chopped
2 teaspoons ginger, chopped
3 teaspoons garlic, crushed
125 ml vegetable oil
310 ml tomato purée
2 tablespoons brown sugar
160 ml boiling water
salt
2 x 750 g mud crabs, cut into pieces
1 egg, beaten
fresh coriander leaves to garnish
serves 4

PREPARATION TIME
10 minutes

COOKING TIME
35 minutes

1 Preheat the oven to 160°C. Pound the chillies, ginger and garlic to a fine paste with a mortar and pestle.

2 Heat the oil in a heavy-bottomed saucepan, add the paste, and cook gently without browning, or until the mixture gives off a spicy aroma.

3 Add tomato purée, brown sugar, 160 ml boiling water and salt, to taste.

4 When sauce is bubbling, place the crab meat into the bottom of a casserole dish and pour over the tomato sauce. Cover, place into the oven and cook for 25 minutes. Remove the lid and quickly stir through the egg, which will become almost scrambled in the sauce.

5 Spoon onto a warmed serving bowl, and sprinkle with coriander leaves. Serve immediately.

NUTRITIONAL VALUE PER SERVE	FAT **24.5** G	CARBOHYDRATE **14** G	PROTEIN **44** G

Octopus with potatoes and peas

INGREDIENTS

1 kg baby octopus, cleaned and
skinned
salt
145 ml olive oil
1 large onion, chopped
4 cloves garlic, chopped
400 g canned tomatoes
¼ teaspoon chilli powder
500 g potatoes, peeled and cut into
thick slices
salt
250 g peas, cooked

serves 4

1 Put octopus in a large saucepan. Sprinkle with salt, cover, and let cook in its own juices over a low heat for about 45 minutes.

2 Four times during the cooking, lift the octopus out with a fork and dip into a pan of boiling water; then run the octopus under cold water and return it to the pan to continue cooking.

3 Heat olive oil in an ovenproof casserole dish and gently fry the onion, garlic, tomatoes and chilli powder for about 10 minutes. Add the potatoes and cook for about 5 minutes. Add the octopus and enough of its cooking liquid to cover the casserole. Add salt as desired. Cook gently, uncovered, for 30 minutes or until the sauce is largely reduced.

4 Finally, add the cooked peas to the casserole and heat through. Serve immediately.

PREPARATION TIME
20 minutes

COOKING TIME
1½ hours

NUTRITIONAL VALUE PER SERVE	FAT 38 G	CARBOHYDRATE 31 G	PROTEIN 72 G

Lobster cheese casserole

INGREDIENTS

500 g lobster meat, diced
2 tablespoons butter
¼ cup plain flour
¾ cup milk
1¼ cups whipping cream
½ cup grated cheddar cheese
½ teaspoon salt
¾ cup green capsicum, diced
¼ cup grated cheddar cheese, extra
pinch paprika

serves 4

1 Preheat the oven to 175°C. Place the lobster in a greased 4 cup casserole dish. In a saucepan over low heat, melt the butter, blend in the flour and slowly add the milk and cream. Cook, stirring constantly, until the mixture is thick and smooth. Add the cheese, salt and capsicum. Stir until the cheese melts.

2 Pour sauce over the lobster. Sprinkle the extra cheese on top and garnish with the paprika. Bake for 15 minutes. Grill for 2 minutes to brown the top and serve.

PREPARATION TIME
10 minutes

COOKING TIME
30 minutes

| NUTRITIONAL VALUE PER SERVE | FAT 42 G | CARBOHYDRATE 9 G | PROTEIN 30 G |

Seafood casserole

INGREDIENTS

1 tablespoon olive oil
1 medium onion, roughly chopped
1 leek, finely chopped
2 cloves garlic, crushed
2 cups canned tomatoes
2 bay leaves
1 tablespoon parsley, chopped
¼ cup dry white wine
salt and freshly ground black pepper
1 kg assorted fish and seafood
2 tablespoons fresh oregano,
  chopped, to garnish

serves 4

PREPARATION TIME
5 minutes

COOKING TIME
35 minutes

1 Heat the oil in a saucepan. Fry the onion, leek and garlic until softened and slightly golden.

2 Add the tomatoes, bay leaves, parsley, wine, salt and pepper. Bring to the boil, cover and simmer gently for 20 minutes.

3 Stir in any firm-fleshed fish and simmer for 5 minutes. Stir in the soft-fleshed fish, placing the shellfish on the top.

4 Cover with a lid and continue cooking for 5–7 minutes until the fish is tender and the shellfish have opened. Discard any that remain closed.

5 Serve garnished with the oregano.

NUTRITIONAL VALUE PER SERVE	FAT 10 G	CARBOHYDRATE 7 G	PROTEIN 50.5 G

Braised vegetables with a cheddar crust

INGREDIENTS

3 tablespoons olive oil
1 tablespoon butter
2 small red onions, thinly sliced
1 head celery, thickly sliced
1 large carrot, thickly sliced
1 clove garlic, crushed
salt and freshly ground black pepper
2 large open mushrooms, sliced
2 red capsicums, cut into strips
1 teaspoon dried oregano
1 teaspoon dried thyme
1 eggplant, thickly sliced
$^{3}/_{4}$ cup vegetable stock
crust
1$^{1}/_{2}$ cups plain flour
1$^{1}/_{2}$ teaspoons baking powder
4 tablespoons chilled butter, cubed
4 tablespoons grated cheddar cheese
2 tablespoons fresh breadcrumbs
$^{1}/_{2}$ cup double cream
2 tablespoons fresh parsley, chopped
1 teaspoon dried oregano
salt and freshly ground black pepper
serves 4

1 Heat 1 tablespoon of the oil with 1 tablespoon of butter in a large frying pan. Add the onions, celery, carrot and garlic. Cook for 10 minutes, stirring often. Season with salt and pepper, remove from the pan and set aside.

2 Preheat the oven to 200°C. Heat another tablespoon of oil in the pan, add the mushrooms, capsicums, oregano and thyme and cook for 5 minutes, stirring often. Season and add to the other vegetables. Heat the remaining oil and fry the eggplant for 3 minutes, turning once, to brown.

3 Add all the vegetables to a greased baking dish, pour in the stock and loosely cover with foil. Cook for 40 minutes. Remove the foil, stir and cook for a further 5 minutes or until tender.

4 Meanwhile, make the crust. Sift the flour and baking powder into a bowl. Rub in the butter. Mix in the cheddar, breadcrumbs, cream, parsley and oregano and season. Increase the oven temperature to 230°C. Spoon the crust mixture over the vegetables. Cook for 20 minutes or until golden. Rest for 10 minutes before serving.

PREPARATION TIME
30 minutes

COOKING TIME
1 hour 35 minutes

NUTRITIONAL VALUE PER SERVE	FAT 45.5 G	CARBOHYDRATE 45 G	PROTEIN 11.5 G

Rich bean and vegetable stew

INGREDIENTS

$^1/_2$ cup dried porcini mushrooms
2$^1/_2$ cups boiling water
3 tablespoons olive oil
1$^1/_2$ cups large open mushrooms, chopped
2 carrots, finely diced
1 large potato, diced
1 cup green beans, chopped
$^1/_2$ tablespoon dried thyme
$^1/_2$ tablespoon dried sage
2 cloves garlic, crushed
1$^1/_2$ cups red wine
2 cups vegetable stock
salt and freshly ground black pepper
1 cup frozen broad beans
1 cup canned cannellini beans
1 cup canned flageolet beans
serves 4

PREPARATION TIME
20 minutes, plus
20 minutes soaking

COOKING TIME
40 minutes

1 Cover the porcini mushrooms with 2$^1/_2$ cups of boiling water, then soak for 20 minutes. Meanwhile, heat the oil in a large saucepan and add the fresh mushrooms, carrots, potato and green beans and gently fry for 3–4 minutes until slightly softened.

2 Add the thyme, sage, garlic, the porcini with their soaking liquid and the wine, stock and seasoning. Bring to the boil, then simmer, uncovered, for 20 minutes or until the vegetables are tender.

3 Stir in the broad beans and simmer for a further 10 minutes or until tender. Drain and rinse the cannellini and flageolet beans, add them to the mixture, then simmer for 2–3 minutes to heat through.

| NUTRITIONAL VALUE PER SERVE | FAT 15 G | CARBOHYDRATE 25 G | PROTEIN 15 G |

Baby vegetable curry with pears

INGREDIENTS

2 tablespoons peanut oil
2 small onions, finely chopped
5 cloves garlic, finely chopped
1 pear, peeled, cored and finely
  chopped
2 tablespoons tomato paste
1 tablespoon mild curry powder
1½ cups vegetable stock
salt and freshly ground black pepper
1 cup baby carrots
1 cup broccoli florets
1½ cups baby cauliflower, quartered
2 tablespoons coriander leaves,
  chopped, to garnish
serves 4

PREPARATION TIME
20 minutes

COOKING TIME
50 minutes

1 Heat the oil in a large, heavy-based saucepan. Add the onions and garlic and fry for 6–8 minutes until golden. Add the pear and fry for a further 6–8 minutes, stirring and scraping the bottom of the pan occasionally until the pear softens and starts to brown. Add a little water if the mixture becomes too dry.

2 Stir in the tomato paste and curry powder and fry for 1–2 minutes to release the flavours. Add the stock, season with salt and pepper and bring to the boil. Reduce the heat and simmer, uncovered, for 15 minutes or until the liquid has slightly reduced.

3 Add the carrots, cover, then simmer for 5 minutes. Add the broccoli and cauliflower, cover, then simmer for a further 10–15 minutes until the vegetables are tender. Serve on a bed of steamed rice and top with coriander.

NUTRITIONAL VALUE PER SERVE   FAT **10** G   CARBOHYDRATE **17** G   PROTEIN **4** G

Glossary

Al dente: Italian term to describe pasta and rice that are cooked until tender but still firm to the bite.

Asafoetida: a herbaceous perennial plant native to Iran. The dried sap is used as a spice. It resembles onion and garlic in flavour.

Bake blind: to bake pastry cases without their fillings. Line the raw pastry case with greaseproof paper and fill with raw rice or dried beans to prevent collapsed sides and puffed base. Remove paper and fill 5 minutes before completion of cooking time.

Baste: to spoon hot cooking liquid over food at intervals during cooking to moisten and flavour it.

Beat: to make a mixture smooth with rapid and regular motions using a spatula, wire whisk or electric mixer; to make a mixture light and smooth by enclosing air.

Beurre manié: equal quantities of butter and flour mixed together to a smooth paste and stirred bit by bit into a soup, stew or sauce while on the heat to thicken. Stop adding when desired thickness results.

Bind: to add egg or a thick sauce to hold ingredients together when cooked.

Blanch: to plunge some foods into boiling water for less than a minute and immediately plunge into iced water. This is to brighten the colour of some vegetables; to remove skin from tomatoes and nuts.

Blend: to mix 2 or more ingredients thoroughly together; do not confuse with blending in an electric blender.

Boil: to cook in a liquid brought to boiling point and kept there.

Boiling point: when bubbles rise continually and break over the entire surface of the liquid, reaching a temperature of 100°C (212°F). In some cases food is held at this high temperature for a few seconds then heat is turned to low for slower cooking. See simmer.

Bouquet garni: a bundle of several herbs tied together with string for easy removal, placed into pots of stock, soups and stews for flavour.

A few sprigs of fresh thyme, parsley and bay leaf are used. Can be purchased in sachet form for convenience.

Caramelise: to heat sugar in a heavy-based pan until it liquefies and develops a caramel colour. Vegetables such as blanched carrots and sautéed onions may be sprinkled with sugar and caramelised.

Chill: to place in the refrigerator or stir over ice until cold.

Clarify: to make a liquid clear by removing sediments and impurities. To melt fat and remove any sediment.

Coat: to dust or roll food items in flour to cover the surface before the food is cooked. Also, to coat in flour, egg and breadcrumbs.

Cool: to stand at room temperature until some or all heat is removed, e.g. cool a little, cool completely.

Cream: to make creamy and fluffy by working the mixture with the back of a wooden spoon, usually refers to creaming butter and sugar or margarine. May also be creamed with an electric mixer.

Croutons: small cubes of bread, toasted or fried, used as an addition to salads or as a garnish to soups and stews.

Crudite: raw vegetable sticks served with a dipping sauce.

Crumb: to coat foods in flour, egg and breadcrumbs to form a protective coating for foods which are fried. Also adds flavour, texture and enhances appearance.

Cube: to cut into small pieces with six even sides, e.g. cubes of meat.

Cut in: to combine fat and flour using 2 knives scissor fashion or with a pastry blender, to make pastry.

Deglaze: to dissolve dried out cooking juices left on the base and sides of a roasting dish or frying pan. Add a little water, wine or stock, scrape and stir over heat until dissolved. Resulting liquid is used to make a flavoursome gravy or added to a sauce or casserole.

Degrease: to skim fat from the surface of cooking liquids, e.g. stocks, soups, casseroles.

Dice: to cut into small cubes.

Dredge: to heavily coat with icing sugar, sugar, flour or cornflour.

Dressing: a mixture added to completed dishes to add moisture and flavour, e.g. salads, cooked vegetables.

Drizzle: to pour in a fine thread-like stream moving over a surface.

Egg wash: beaten egg with milk or water used to brush over pastry, bread dough or biscuits to give a sheen and golden brown colour.

Essence: a strong flavouring liquid, usually made by distillation. Only a few drops are needed to flavour.

Fillet: a piece of prime meat, fish or poultry which is boneless or has all bones removed.

Flake: to separate cooked fish into flakes, removing any bones and skin, using 2 forks.

Flame: to ignite warmed alcohol over food or to pour into a pan with food, ignite then serve.

Flute: to make decorative indentations around the pastry rim before baking.

Fold in: combining of a light, whisked or creamed mixture with other ingredients. Add a portion of the other ingredients at a time and mix using a gentle circular motion, over and under the mixture so that air will not be lost. Use a silver spoon or spatula.

Glaze: to brush or coat food with a liquid that will give the finished product a glossy appearance, and on baked products, a golden brown colour.

Grease: to rub the surface of a metal or heatproof dish with oil or fat, to prevent the food from sticking.

Herbed butter: softened butter mixed with finely chopped fresh herbs and re-chilled. Used to serve on grilled meats and fish.

Hors d'oeuvre: small savoury foods served as an appetiser, popularly known today as 'finger food'.

Infuse: to steep foods in a liquid until the liquid absorbs their flavour.

Joint: to cut poultry and game into serving pieces by dividing at the joint.

Julienne: to cut some food, e.g. vegetables and processed meats, into fine strips the length of matchsticks. Used for inclusion in salads or as a garnish to cooked dishes.

Knead: to work a yeast dough in a pressing, stretching and folding motion with the heel of the hand until smooth and elastic to develop the gluten strands. Non-yeast doughs should be lightly and quickly handled as gluten development is not desired.

Line: to cover the inside of a baking tin with paper for the easy removal of the cooked product from the baking tin.

Macerate: to stand fruit in a syrup, liqueur or spirit to give added flavour.

Marinade: a flavoured liquid, into which food is placed for some time to give it flavour and to tenderise. Marinades include an acid ingredient such as vinegar or wine, oil and seasonings.

Mask: to evenly cover cooked food portions with a sauce, mayonnaise or savoury jelly.

Pan-fry: to fry foods in a small amount of fat or oil, sufficient to coat the base of the pan.

Parboil: to boil until partially cooked. The food is then finished by some other method.

Pare: to peel the skin from vegetables and fruit. Peel is the popular term but pare is the name given to the knife used; paring knife.

Pit: to remove stones or seeds from olives, cherries, dates.

Pith: the white lining between the rind and flesh of oranges, grapefruit and lemons.

Pitted: the olives, cherries, dates etc. with the stone removed, e.g. purchase pitted dates.

Poach: to simmer gently in enough hot liquid to almost cover the food so shape will be retained.

Pound: to flatten meats with a meat mallet; to reduce to a paste or small particles with a mortar and pestle.

Simmer: to cook in liquid just below boiling point at about 96°C (205°F) with small bubbles rising gently to the surface.

Skim: to remove fat or froth from the surface of simmering food.

Stock: the liquid produced when meat, poultry, fish or vegetables have been simmered in water to extract the flavour. Used as a base for soups, sauces, casseroles etc. Convenience stock products are available.

Sweat: to cook sliced onions or vegetables, in a small amount of butter in a covered pan over low heat, to soften them and release flavour without colouring.

Conversions

Measurements differ from country to country, so it's important to understand what the differences are. This Measurements Guide gives you simple 'at-a-glance' information for using the recipes in this book, wherever you may be.

Cooking is not an exact science – minor variations in measurements won't make a difference to your cooking.

EQUIPMENT

There is a difference in the size of measuring cups used internationally, but the difference is minimal (only 2–3 teaspoons). We use the Australian standard metric measurements in our recipes:

1 teaspoon ....5 ml	1 tablespoon....20 ml
1/2 cup......125 ml	1 cup.....250 ml
4 cups...1 litre	

Measuring cups come in sets of one cup (250 ml), 1/2 cup (125 ml), 1/3 cup (80 ml) and 1/4 cup (60 ml). Use these for measuring liquids and certain dry ingredients.

Measuring spoons come in a set of four and should be used for measuring dry and liquid ingredients.

When using cup or spoon measures always make them level (unless the recipe indicates otherwise).

DRY VERSUS WET INGREDIENTS

While this system of measures is consistent for liquids, it's more difficult to quantify dry ingredients. For instance, one level cup equals: 200 g of brown sugar; 210 g of caster sugar; and 110 g of icing sugar.

When measuring dry ingredients such as flour, don't push the flour down or shake it into the cup. It is best just to spoon the flour in until it reaches the desired amount. When measuring liquids use a clear vessel indicating metric levels.

Always use medium eggs (55–60 g) when eggs are required in a recipe.

OVEN

Your oven should always be at the right temperature before placing the food in it to be cooked. Note that if your oven doesn't have a fan you may need to cook food for a little longer.

MICROWAVE

It is difficult to give an exact cooking time for microwave cooking. It is best to watch what you are cooking closely to monitor its progress.

STANDING TIME

Many foods continue to cook when you take them out of the oven or microwave. If a recipe states that the food needs to 'stand' after cooking, be sure not to overcook the dish.

CAN SIZES

The can sizes available in your supermarket or grocery store may not be the same as specified in the recipe. Don't worry if there is a small variation in size – it's unlikely to make a difference to the end result.

dry		liquids	
metric (grams)	imperial (ounces)	metric (millilitres)	imperial (fluid ounces)
		30 ml	1 fl oz
30 g	1 oz	60 ml	2 fl oz
60 g	2 oz	90 ml	3 fl oz
90 g	3 oz	100 ml	3 1/2 fl oz
100 g	3 1/2 oz	125 ml	4 fl oz
125 g	4 oz	150 ml	5 fl oz
150 g	5 oz	190 ml	6 fl oz
185 g	6 oz	250 ml	8 fl oz
200 g	7 oz	300 ml	10 fl oz
250 g	8 oz	500 ml	16 fl oz
280 g	9 oz	600 ml	20 fl oz (1 pint)*
315 g	10 oz	1000 ml (1 litre)	32 fl oz
330 g	11 oz		
370 g	12 oz		
400 g	13 oz		
440 g	14 oz		
470 g	15 oz		
500 g	16 oz (1 lb)		
750 g	24 oz (1 1/2 lb)		
1000 g (1 kg)	32 oz (2 lb)		*Note: an American pint is 16 fl oz.

cooking temperatures	°C (celsius)	°F (fahrenheit)	gas mark
very slow	120	250	1/2
slow	150	300	2
moderately slow	160	315	2–3
moderate	180	350	4
moderate hot	190	375	5
	200	400	6
hot	220	425	7
very hot	230	450	8
	240	475	9
	250	500	10

Index